Read and Play
Planes

by Jim Pipe

Aladdin/Watts
London · Sydney

plane

2

This is a **plane**.

A **plane** can fly.

wings

A plane
has **wings**.

4

Wings help a plane fly.

5

wheels

6

A plane has **wheels**.

Wheels roll along a runway.

7

engine

8

This plane has a jet **engine**.

propeller

This plane has a **propeller**.

9

pilot

10

This plane has two **pilots**.

A **pilot** flies a plane.

airport

This is
an **airport**.

12

A plane lands at an **airport**.

13

jumbo

14

A **jumbo** is a big plane.

It carries lots of people.

short

This plane has **short** wings.

long

This plane has **long** wings.

17

sea

18   A **sea** plane lands on water.

stunt

This plane does **stunts**.

19

What am I?

wheels

wing

pilot

engine

20 Match the words and pictures.

How many?

Can you count the planes?

21

Look up!

balloon

butterfly

helicopter

bird

Look in the sky. What else can fly?

Index

Can you find these
pictures of planes
in the book?

For Parents and Teachers

Questions you could ask:

p.2 What can you see in this picture? e.g. clouds in background. Many passenger planes fly high in the sky, above the clouds.

p. 4 What else has wings? e.g. flying animals such as birds, bees and butterflies.

p. 6 Can you see the runway? A runway is a hard, smooth surface for the plane to land on. Ask: What if a plane landed on a soft or bumpy surface?

p. 8 Where are the engines on these planes? e.g. jet engine is on the wing, propeller engine is at front of plane. Spot engines on other planes in the book.

p. 10 Where do pilots sit? In the cockpit (usually at front). Point out cockpits on other planes in the book.

p. 12 What is happening in this picture? e.g. plane refuelling and baggage being loaded. People get on to the plane using a walkway (see picture) or stairs.

p. 14 How big do you think this plane is? Compare the plane with person standing on the runway.

p. 17 What is unusual about this plane? It does not have an engine. A glider has long wings to help it glide like a bird. Another plane pulls it into the air.

p. 18 What is different about these two planes? e.g. floats/wheels, number of wings, pilot inside/outside.

p. 20 Who am I? If they need a clue, children can look back to pages 4, 6, 8 and 10.

Activities you could do:

• Ask the reader to draw a simple plane, writing labels for wings, engine, wheels, cockpit, cabin.

• Ask the reader to act out how a plane or bird moves through the sky. Encourage them to make the appropriate noises if they know them.

• Ask the reader to describe a flight they might like to go on, e.g. what happens at take-off.

• You could help the reader to fold paper into a dart to show how a glider flies.

• Build a plane mobile using plane shapes cut from card and painted. Mobiles can be made using criss-cross straws tied with wool or string.

© Aladdin Books Ltd 2006

Designed and produced by
Aladdin Books Ltd
2/3 Fitzroy Mews
London W1T 6DF

First published in 2006
by Franklin Watts
338 Euston Road,
London NW1 3BH

Franklin Watts Australia
Hachette Children's Books
Level 17/207 Kent Street
Sydney NSW 2000

ISBN 0 7496 6870 9

A catalogue record for this book is available from the British Library.

Dewey Classification: 629.133 ' 34

Printed in Malaysia

All rights reserved

Series consultant
Zoe Stillwell is an experienced Early Years teacher currently teaching at Pewley Down Infant School, Guildford.

Photocredits:
l-left, r-right, b-bottom, t-top, c-centre, m-middle
All photos from istockphoto.com except: 4-5, 23br — British Airways copyright images. 6-7 — US Navy. 10-11, 20br, 22tl & bl — Corbis. 14-15, 23bl – Airbus. 23br – Stockbyte. 22tr — Otto Rogge Photography.